AF131413

BOOK ANALYSIS

By Gus Mitchell

As You Like It

by William Shakespeare

WILLIAM SHAKESPEARE

ENGLISH PLAYWRIGHT AND POET

- **Born in Stratford-upon-Avon in 1564.**
- **Died in Stratford-upon-Avon in 1616.**
- **Notable works:**
  - *King Lear* (1623), play
  - *A Midsummer Night's Dream* (1600), play
  - *Richard III* (1597), play

William Shakespeare was an English playwright and poet and is generally considered the most influential writer in the English language. He worked in several modes including comedy, history, tragedy, the narrative poem and the sonnet, and was active during an extraordinary flowering of creativity during the Elizabethan Renaissance – not just as a playwright, but also as an actor and as the eventual co-owner of the Globe theatre in London. Shakespeare spent 20 years in London, where he wrote all of his famous works and staged them with his own acting company, The King's Men, and others. Shakespeare's plays are universal in their scope, as they explore all the complexities of the human experience, from politics to love and death. Played constantly all around the world and revered for their complex characters and deft use of language, Shakespeare's plays are now considered one of the crowning jewels of English and international literary heritage.

AS YOU LIKE IT

COMIC DRAMA

- **Genre:** play
- **Reference edition:** Shakespeare, W. (2004) *As You Like It*. London: The Arden Shakespeare, ed. by Juliet Dusinberre.
- **1st edition:** 1623
- **Themes:** love, pastoral life vs. city life, injustice, forgiveness, cleverness and foolishness, gender, culture, philosophy and thought

Written around 1599 and first published in the First Folio edition of 1623, *As You Like It* is one of Shakespeare's most well-known and beloved comedies. The heroine of *As You Like It*, a young woman called Rosalind, flees a bad situation in the court of her uncle, a French duke, and into the strange Forest of Arden, where she encounters a young man called Orlando and a host of other strange characters. The play is firmly in the 'pastoral' tradition; that is, it takes place in natural and rural settings while promoting a somewhat idyllic view of a life away from the bustle of human activity in a city or a court. However, as always with Shakespeare, this is complicated by the fact that he includes characters who almost parody the earnest pastoral tradition, and thereby is also writing a kind of wry satirical take on the genre. Despite this, *As You Like It* is also one of Shakespeare's most hopeful comedies, one which seems to challenge the restrictions and lack of freedoms, particularly of women, in the England of Shakespeare's age.

SUMMARY

ONE FATHER DEAD AND ONE FATHER BANISHED

The wealthy Sir Rowland de Bois has died, and his inheritance legally passes to his eldest son, Oliver. According to his will, Oliver must take good care of his younger (and more beloved) brother, Orlando. Instead, Oliver spites Orlando by denying him the privileges of his upbringing which would allow him to grow into a gentleman.

As the play opens Orlando is complaining to his servant Adam that his education and his property are being kept from him. Oliver enters and Orlando tells him of his anger, with Oliver quickly assuring him that things will be rectified.

When Orlando leaves, Charles, a prize wrestler, enters with the news that Orlando is challenging him to fight the next day, but he wishes to avoid the bout since he is reluctant to strike a nobleman and he fears he will kill Orlando. Oliver gleefully lies to Charles, saying that he has tried to dissuade his brother but in vain, and that Orlando will most likely resort to dirty play to win. Charles leaves determined to beat Orlando. Oliver delivers a soliloquy revealing his deep hatred for Orlando.

Charles also delivered the news to Oliver that his master, Duke Frederick, has usurped the Duchy from his own elder brother. Rosalind, the daughter of the exiled Duke, has remained at the court with her friend Celia, Frederick's daughter, while Rosalind's father has retreated to the Forest of Arden, living like a Robin Hood with a loyal band of supporters. Among them, the most prominent in the story is Jaques, a melancholic lord who delivers philosophical speeches to the rest.

A WRESTLING MATCH AND TWO BANISHMENTS

The scene now moves to Frederick's court, where Celia consoles Rosalind over her father's exile and tries to convince her that her own father, the new Duke, can be a father to them both. The wrestling match is announced, and Rosalind and

Celia beg Orlando to withdraw, but he refuses. To the amazement of all, Orlando beats Charles. Orlando and Rosalind have also fallen in love at first sight.

Duke Frederick orders Rosalind to leave his court on pain of death. Celia promises Rosalind that they will be exiled together, and they plan to leave with Touchstone, the court fool. Rosalind will dress like a man (Ganymede) and Celia a shepherdess (Aliena), and they will go find Rosalind's father the real Duke (Duke Senior) in the Forest of Arden. Orlando has also returned home, only to be warned by Adam that Oliver's plot against Orlando's life is serious and he intends to burn down the house with Orlando inside. He tells Orlando he must seek exile and offers to go with him. They too head to the Forest of Arden.

Duke Frederick discovers Celia is missing and, suspecting that Orlando is with the two girls, decides that Oliver shall lead the manhunt, on pain of losing his titles and property if he fails. He also decides he must end his brother's existence once and for all and decides to raise an army to stamp him and his forest followers out.

INTO THE FOREST OF ARDEN

Meanwhile, in the Forest of Arden, we meet the exiled Duke praising the simple pleasures of life among nature, away from the difficulties and scheming of the court. The group are interrupted by Orlando, who, believing he must act tough, demands food for himself and Adam, who is by now starving. Duke Senior learns that Orlando is the son of his former close friend Sir Rowland and warmly invites him and Adam to join them.

During this time Rosalind, Celia and Touchstone have been making their own way through the forest, and now encounter Silvius and Corin. Silvius is a pining young lover who despairs of winning his beloved, the distant Phebe, while Corin, an old man, tries to talk him round. Rosalind and Celia are also hungry but Corin has nothing to offer, although he mentions that an adjacent cottage, with its livestock and pasture, are for sale. The girls spontaneously decide to buy it and set up their abode in the forest there.

ROSALIND AND ORLANDO MEET; TOUCHSTONE AND AUDREY IN LOVE

Soon Rosalind, dressed as Ganymede, runs into the unknowing Orlando, who, lovesick for her, has been dedicating poems to her on the trees. Celia has revealed to Rosalind that the author of the poems is Orlando, and she brings this up when talking to him. Orlando admits that he is author, to which Rosalind responds that she is a master in curing love and offers to cure Orlando of his affliction by acting as a terrible version of Rosalind. She will only do this if he agrees to come wooing her every day.

A subplot involves Touchstone falling in love with and getting engaged to the silly shepherdess Audrey. They are in the midst of arguing about Audrey's inability to be romantic and poetic enough for Touchstone when a curate arrives to marry them. Touchstone, however, wishes to be married in a church and changes his mind; he must also soon vie with William, another shepherd, for Audrey's affection.

SILVIUS LOVES PHEBE; PHEBE LOVES GANYMEDE; OLIVER LOVES CELIA; ORLANDO SAVES OLIVER

Phebe continues to reject Silvius, and Rosalind and Celia witness one particularly bad encounter between the two. Rosalind (still dressed as the man Ganymede) intervenes with Phebe and insultingly berates her for her conduct, whereat Phebe falls deeply in love with him/her.

One day Orlando does not show up for his lesson in love with Rosalind. Oliver arrives on the scene with a bloody napkin, sent by Orlando, who was saving his brother from being eaten by a lioness when he came across him in the forest. Rosalind faints.

Meanwhile, Phebe's pursuit of "Ganymede" has become ever more insistent, and she is sending "him" love letters. Orlando is growing tired of pretending that "Ganymede" is Rosalind. Meanwhile, Oliver, who is in the forest to search for Orlando and has subsequently been saved by him from the lioness, tells his brother that he has fallen in love with Celia, who he of course believes is the shepherdess, Aliena. She reciprocates his feelings.

FOUR MARRIAGES AND DUKE SENIOR IS RESTORED

The confusion of multiplying love triangles comes to a head when Silvius, Phebe, Rosalind/Ganymede and Orlando come to argue over who will get to marry whom. Rosalind decides to end the playacting and tells Orlando that she will use magic to make sure that Orlando marries Rosalind tomorrow, if he loves her truly. She lays out all of the unions to take place the next day: Orlando, Silvius and Ganymede (herself) will all be married. Orlando will marry Rosalind, while Rosalind as Ganymede will marry Phebe if he ever marries a woman. If Phebe does not get to marry Ganymede by tomorrow, then she will marry Silvius. All the parties agree.

The wedding day arrives, and Rosalind gathers the various couples to fulfil her master plan: Phebe/Silvius, Touchstone/Audrey, Oliver/Celia, and Orlando. The group gather again with Duke Senior and his followers. Rosalind gets Phebe to swear that should she suddenly not want to marry Ganymede, she will instead marry Silvius. She also secures a promise from Duke Senior (her father, though unbeknownst to him while she is in disguise) that he would allow his daughter to wed Orlando. Rosalind and Celia then exit and reappear out of their disguises, accompanied by Hymen, the god of marriage. Hymen accompanies Rosalind to greet her father and Orlando, whom she marries; Phebe agrees to marry Silvius, just as Rosalind designed. Hymen then brings together in marriage the remaining two couples: Oliver and Celia and Touchstone and Audrey.

At this moment, Jaques de Bois (the third of Sir Rowland's sons after Oliver and Orlando) enters the scene and informs the gathered company that Duke Frederick, on his way to kill his elder brother the Duke in the forest once and for all, instead encountered a holy man and converted to a religious life of peace. He has decided to return his usurped titles and lands to Duke Senior, to which the Duke responds with happiness and suggests that they celebrate the good occasion by continuing with the marriage ceremonies.

The Duke's companion, the melancholy Jaques, states that he will not be returning to the court, but instead will stay in the forest and follow Frederick's lead in a religious, monastic life. Rosalind delivers an epilogue to the audience to end the play.

CHARACTER STUDY

ROSALIND

Rosalind is the heroine and standout star of As You Like It. She is considered one of Shakespeare's most defined creations and strongest female characters. Her subtle and complex ability to read and communicate her own thoughts and emotions, as well as those of the other people in the play, marks her out from everybody around her. Even the intelligent, melancholy and perceptive Jaques and the witty Touchstone come up short next to her in entertainment value.

Rosalind is a critic in the widest and deepest sense – she observes the world and the people around her and makes judgments on them, and changes things along the way. However, unlike Jaques, who is perhaps an example of the critic's impulse gone too far and tipping into a cynical impotence, Rosalind throws herself into the world and influences it with her energy and intelligence.

But Shakespeare also thinks to throw in many touches which humanise her to us, making her more than merely a super-smart mastermind: she can be difficult and throw tantrums, such as when Orlando is late for their "lesson", only to faint in horror at the sight of his blood.

Rosalind is often seen as a proto-feminist character in Shakespeare's canon, given her determination to live in her own way and defy the restrictions which are imposed on her as a woman. She and Celia make a self-sufficient life for themselves in the forest, and instruct men (Orlando, Silvius, Touchstone) in the ways of love – all while being disguised as men themselves.

Shakespeare himself was clearly aware of the divergence of her behaviour from accepted "female" norms, and the fact that she becomes only an actor again in her spoken epilogue seems to be a placatory gesture to contemporary concerns and a way of showing that this whole permissive world has only been a fantasy, a play, which they are now exiting. However, the example that Rosalind, in her freedom and her wisdom regarding herself and others, has set lingers on.

ORLANDO

Orlando's strongest qualities are his nobility and generosity of spirit, and though he has plenty of wit, he cannot hold a candle to Rosalind. He inspires great love in most people he meets, which is something even Oliver admits, in his soliloquy in the first scene. His naivety and lack of awareness about himself and his relationships make him a foil for Rosalind during their love lessons. A story in which the hero is naïve and un-tutored, and the heroine is all-knowing and in control constitutes a rare role reversal in the gender politics of Elizabethan theatre.

Yet Orlando and Rosalind are one of Shakespeare's most appealing and well-matched couples because they both possess all the right virtues when placed together. Orlando performs many worthy acts throughout the story, such as his furious attempts to feed Adam, his aged travelling companion, and risking his life to save the brother who has betrayed him in the past. Orlando's journey is also an interesting comment by Shakespeare on pastoralism. Although Orlando complains at the beginning of the play about being denied the education and privileges to make him a gentleman, his experiences proving himself out in the unsophisticated, natural environment of Arden have made him a worthy character by the play's conclusion.

TOUCHSTONE

Touchstone, as a Shakespearian fool, has plenty of wittiness and silliness to spare. However, like Rosalind, he is at his core a perceptive judge of other peoples' characters. This quality is in line with his profession of "fool" – think of Lear's Fool as another, more serious example. However, he is again a foil for Rosalind, since most of his pronouncements seem graceless and even vulgar compared to the fine-tipped precision she exhibits.

OLIVER

Oliver is plagued by an irrational hatred of his younger brother Orlando. Their relationship is an interesting mirror for the other fraternal relationship in the play, that of Duke Frederick and Duke Senior, wherein the younger brother usurps and steals the rights of the elder and exiles him.

Although Oliver admits that he does not know you can take this out if you want why he hates his brother so much, one might speculate that it is a matter of disproportionate paternal love, given that at the beginning of the play their father has just died, leaving Oliver in control of the estate and with total power over his brother's future. Like Duke Frederick, Oliver transforms into a more loving person through his experiences in the Forest of Arden, far removed from the greed and mendacity of the court and the city. He even falls in love with Celia, who he believes to be a poor shepherdess, further demonstrating the change in his character for the better.

DUKE SENIOR

The exiled and usurped Duke Senior seems to be a fairly easy-going man who accepts what life brings him and seems not unhappy to have found a harmonious and peaceful refuge in the Forest of Arden with his companions. However, unlike his daughter Rosalind, he is fairly clueless about the character and motivations of others, evidenced by his apparent lack of fight to keep his dukedom and his inability to perceive his brother's treacherous nature until it was too late (one cannot imagine Rosalind doing either of those things). He is a peaceful soul and has much to learn and enjoy from the pastoral life, saying that he gains as much wisdom from stones and running waters as in a church, library or court. However, although, like Orlando, he is no match for his daughter in terms of wit, he is a kind and generous ruler, and is happy for her to be wed to the man she loves at the end of the play.

DUKE FREDERICK

Duke Frederick seems to be an implacable villain at the beginning of the play. A tyrannical and power-hungry ruler, he seems to exercise his power capriciously, purely to show that he can, and to have a very irrational temper, shown when he banishes Rosalind from the court without giving a reason. However, the Duke's character, apparently so unredeemable, is changed for the better upon meeting a holy man in the forest (while on his way with his army to finally murder his brother). While this sudden change of heart may for some audiences or critics have too great a touch of the implausible *deus ex machina*, it could also be seen as Shakespeare's way of showing, in this idealised, pastoral world of *As You Like It*, that sometimes apparently fallen men can indeed change for the better.

JAQUES

One of Duke Senior's faithful lords and companions, Jaques is melancholic, a disposition which was discussed and taken seriously in Shakespeare's day as a partly medical condition. In many ways, Jaques would also be seen in contemporary terms as a depressive. Like Rosalind, he observes the world and those around him with a keen eye and wit, but unlike her, he allows his musings to drag him down into a cynical, enclosed worldview which he expounds upon in his occasional, famous speeches to the rest of the company. He is even inspired by meeting Touchstone to believe that he should become a professional fool, so that his cynical, discerning wit can find some use in the world. However, while the fool might find be inadvertently useful to himself and others through his wit (just as Rosalind is), Jaques merely constructs a solipsism from which he finds it difficult to engage meaningfully with the world. This disposition eventually finds its only outlet when he decides that he will join Duke Frederick in a monastery and live a life of holy remove from the rest of the world.

ANALYSIS

BACKGROUND AND CONTEXT

As You Like It was probably written between 1598 and 1599, and around that time Shakespeare had recently proved his gifts as a timeless dramatist with works like *A Midsummer Night's Dream* and *Romeo and Juliet*, as well as composing *Hamlet* roughly contemporaneously. This was perhaps the most consistently productive and brilliant time in Shakespeare's writing life. The dark, ambiguous vision of the world which emerges in *Hamlet* is answered by *As You Like It*'s predominantly positive tone and feel: the one character who tries to act like he is in a tragic play, Jaques, is not taken very seriously by Shakespeare, while all of the play's villains are redeemed by their own realisations of what they have done wrong. It is one of Shakespeare's most harmonious and optimistic visions of the world, although it is certainly (as Rosalind acknowledges in her Epilogue) an idealistic one.

As You Like It is classed as one of Shakespeare's comedies; that is, it includes the following: mostly young and confused people falling in love; a great deal of punning and linguistic humour; musical and poetic interludes straying from the actual plot; and the (as-yet unfulfilled) promise of marriages and happy endings at the conclusion.

The play also has strong elements of the pastoral, an ancient poetic tradition which was very popular during the English Renaissance, with roots that can be traced as far back as Ancient Greece. Pastorals take place in, or sing the praises of, a rustic, innocent countryside, and extol the virtues of people with a strong connection to nature and the land. Shakespeare's pastorals especially were often set up as contrasts to the mendacious, scheming and mentally draining life of the courtier or the insider, those forced to make their way in the domain of nobles and kings, rather than the simplicity of natural law.

Like most of Shakespeare's works, *As You Like It*'s story is taken from pre-existing sources. The most obvious of these is *Rosalynde, Euphues Golden Legacie* by Thomas Lodge, published in 1590 and based upon "The Tale of Gamelyn", a Middle English tale sometimes wrongly attributed to Geoffrey Chaucer. From this Shakespeare took the sentimental and pastoral setting and the plots involving intertwined love interests. It seems that he added the two "fools" characters in the play, Touchstone and Jaques.

The play's pastoral setting is largely the Forest of Arden, which is a real forest in England, close to Shakespeare's home town, Stratford-upon-Avon. Arden was also Shakespeare's mother's maiden name. However, given the setting at the French court, it is more likely Shakespeare had the French Arden Wood, which features heavily in the Italian epics *Orlando Innamorato* and *Orlando Furioso*, in mind. The fact that the Shakespeare named his romantic hero Orlando supports this theory. In the myths, the Arden Wood hides Merlin's Fountain, whose waters cause people to fall out of love. Thomas Lodge, Shakespeare's main source, also set his tale in the Ardennes region of France, and it is also possible that Arden is Shakespeare's anglicisation of the region. The question is in another sense irrelevant, given that pastoral settings are often fantasy-based and precise details are not important.

It is useful to remember that Shakespeare's period was Elizabethan England, a deeply rigid, class-based and patriarchal society. Women's rights, including their right to choose who they married, were largely non-existent It is no surprise that marrying for love, seen as foolish and impractical in the real world, was largely the domain of imaginative literature such as the plays of Shakespeare. The strangely free and egalitarian world of *As You Like It*, at least in the more idealistic realm of the Forest of Arden, reflects the desire for a less pre-determined world, where the character and intelligence displayed by people influences their fate more than their class or sex. In *As You Like It*, the search for love in marriage is paramount, as is escape from the rigid rules of the court and the freedom to live side-by-side with nature's laws.

LOVE

Being a Shakespearian comedy, romantic love is the most prominent theme of *As You Like It*. Shakespeare explores many different kinds of love and its manifestations: the love at first sight of Rosalind, Orlando, Oliver and Phebe; Silvius's undignified devotion to Phebe, who does not love him; Orlando's terrible love poetry. Shakespeare allows every exaggerated aspect of love to play out with humorous results, mocking the drama and performativity with which people approach the idea of "being in love".

A great deal of courtly love poetry in the Renaissance featured/drew on the pastoral themes and imagery also present in *As You Like It*. Shakespeare is lampooning several of these tropes here, such as the male lover who becomes the devoted "slave" of his mistress, as in Silvius's case. Orlando's poems typically announce that he must "live and die [Rosalind's] slave", and she ridicules him for them (III.ii.142). It is perhaps part of Shakespeare's modernisation of the ideas surrounding love that he makes fun of these centuries-old tropes and foregrounds Rosalind as the play's most effective lover, the others relying on her to actually put their desires into effect.

"Men have died from time to time, and worms have eaten them, but not for love," Rosalind declares, showing her impatience with the image of the moping, despairing lover (IV.i.91-2). For Rosalind, the business of attaining and retaining love should be practical and based on happiness, not on tormenting oneself with artificial, self-important posturing. Both Jaques and Touchstone have the fool's sharp wit when talking about and against love, but Rosalind wishes to communicate and spread love which brings happiness, and it seems that Shakespeare definitely intends us to take her side. This determined, practical striving after the positive, desired outcome in relationships is surely implied in the play's title – 'As You Like It'.

PASTORALISM AND URBANISM

The pastoral tradition in Western literature is as old as Ancient Greek poetry and the odes of Theocritus in the 3rd century BCE. The most common themes in pastoralism are a rural or natural setting, and the implied innocence in lifestyle and attitude implied by that as preferable to the complexities of city and court life. Pastoralism in drama became popular during Shakespeare's lifetime, in the second half of the 16th century.

Gradually, the idea of the idyllic pastoral setting developed out of combinations of the classically-derived region of Arcadia and the biblical Eden.

Similarly, *As You Like It* features combinations of classical and Christian motifs, such as the Greek god of marriage, Hymen, officiating with apparently Christian characters in an apparently contemporary world. This kind of dissolving of boundaries and blurring of worlds is typical of the freedom and lack of boundaries promised by a pastoral setting.

Shakespeare complicates things, of course. His addition of Touchstone, Jaques and Audrey to Thomas Lodge's original story all indicate that he is playing with the boundaries of how people are supposed to act in a pastoral mode. Touchstone's acerbic wit never abates even when in the supposedly cleansing environment of the forest; Jaques, too, merely uses the forest as a canvas on which to project his blinkered view of humankind's place in the world, not as a means of redemption or perspective on how to live better. Touchstone's love interest Audrey, meanwhile, is an inarticulate and unappealing girl, though she lives in the forest, removed from the alleged impurities of the court and city.

Shakespeare's investigation of the power of the pastoral ideal is nuanced, partaking of a complex mix of scepticism and optimism. Despite the above-mentioned playing with pastoral convention, he does certainly set the forest up early on as a cure for the unhappiness people inflict on one another. Orlando leaves the question begging when he bemoans his Oliver's unjust treatment of him and complains that he "know[s] no wise remedy how to avoid it" (I.i.20-21). And later in the same scene, Charles the wrestler gives us an image of the forest as place where "many young gentlemen [...] fleet the time carelessly, as they did in the golden world" (I.i.99-103). Images of the perfect worlds of Eden or the Greek Golden Age are also bound into the pastoral idea.

While the Forest of Arden does indeed fulfil Shakespeare's promise to make things more perfect – the lovers' difficulties are solved by marriages, the two villains repent by their own will, justice is restored between the brothers – the characters' eagerness to return to the court with things put to rights does not suggest that a life lived always in the forest is desirable or realistic. Rather, the pastoral life may be part of a necessary balance in human life, by which perspective can be gained and freedoms realised.

Destructive, anti-social behaviours have been rooted out and hopefully cured, and a fresh, wiser return to the city and the court can now take place.

FURTHER REFLECTION

SOME QUESTIONS TO THINK ABOUT...

- Do you believe Rosalind might be a character of whom Shakespeare was particularly fond? If so, why? If not, why not?
- In your opinion, is Orlando an interesting hero? Does he seem intelligent or not?
- Do you find it unrealistic or fitting that Duke Frederick suddenly sees the error of his ways upon meeting a holy man in the forest?
- Imagine you are staging this play and have been told to make it as contemporary as possible. What directorial choices would you make? What might you do with the text? Would you cut anything, and if so what?
- Are there many similarities between *As You Like It* and Shakespeare's other comedies, or his other work in general? What seems specific and unique about this play?
- Who do you think is the play's funniest character? Why?

- Why do you think Shakespeare included the character of Jaques, who is so incidental to the central plot, and gave him so much speaking time?
- Why do you think this play has a reputation as a crowd-pleaser?
- What reasons can you think of that the play's reputation with critics has been mixed?

We want to hear from you!
Leave a comment on your online library
and share your favourite books on social media!

FURTHER READING

REFERENCE EDITION

- Shakespeare, W. (2004) *As You Like It*. London: The Arden Shakespeare, ed. by Juliet Dusinberre.

REFERENCE STUDIES

- Gay, P. (2012) *The Cambridge Introduction to Shakespeare's Comedies*. Cambridge: Cambridge University Press.

- Smith, E. ed. (2003) *Shakespeare's Comedies: A Guide to Criticism*. London: Blackwell Publishing.

- McDonald, R. ed. (2004) *Shakespeare: An Anthology of Criticism and Theory*. London: John Wiley & Sons.

ADAPTATIONS

- *As You Like It*. (2007) [Film]. Kenneth Branagh. *Dir. UK: Lionsgate.*

MORE FROM BRIGHTSUMMARIES.COM

- Reading guide – *A Midsummer Night's Dream* by William Shakespeare.

- Reading guide – *All's Well That Ends Well* by William Shakespeare.

- Reading guide – *Antony and Cleopatra* by William Shakespeare.

- Reading guide – *Coriolanus* by William Shakespeare.

- Reading guide – *Hamlet* by William Shakespeare.

- Reading guide – *Julius Caesar* by William Shakespeare.

- Reading guide – *King Lear* by William Shakespeare.

- Reading guide – *Love's Labour's Lost* by William Shakespeare.

- Reading guide – *Macbeth* by William Shakespeare.

- Reading guide – *Measure for Measure* by William Shakespeare.

- Reading guide – *Much Ado About Nothing* by William Shakespeare.

- Reading guide – *Othello* by William Shakespeare.

- Reading guide – *Richard III* by William Shakespeare.

- Reading guide – *Romeo and Juliet* by William Shakespeare.

- Reading guide – *The Merchant of Venice* by William Shakespeare.

- Reading guide – *The Taming of the Shrew* by William Shakespeare.

- Reading guide – *The Tempest* by William Shakespeare.

- Reading guide – *The Two Gentlemen of Verona* by William Shakespeare.

- Reading guide – *The Winter's Tale* by William Shakespeare.

- Reading guide – *Titus Andronicus* by William Shakespeare.

- Reading guide – *Troilus and Cressida* by William Shakespeare.

- Reading guide – *Twelfth Night* by William Shakespeare.

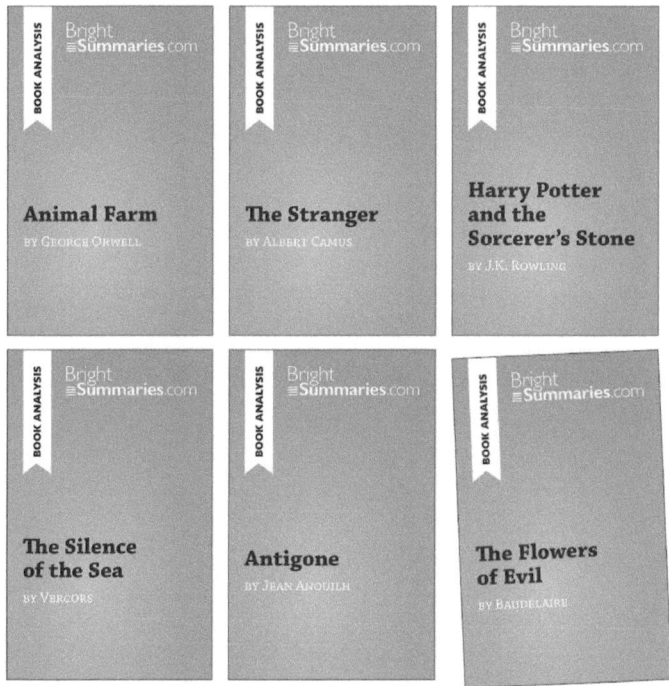

www.brightsummaries.com

Ebook EAN: 9782808018739

Paperback EAN: 9782808018746

Legal Deposit: D/2019/12603/103

Cover: © Primento

Digital conception by Primento, the digital partner of publishers.